ON THE JOB
Creative Careers

# Be a FASHION DESIGNER!

Theresa Emminizer

PowerKiDS press.

Published in 2025 by The Rosen Publishing Group, Inc.
2544 Clinton Street, Buffalo, NY 14224



First Edition

Editor: Theresa Emminizer
Book Design: Michael Flynn

Photo Credits: Cover Amnaj Khetsamtip/Shutterstock.com; (series background) KanokpolTokumhnerd/Shutterstock.com; (series boxes) vector illustration/Shutterstock.com; p. 4 REDPIXEL.PL/Shutterstock.com; p. 5 Tatyana Vyc/Shutterstock.com; p. 7 Media_Photos/Shutterstock.com; p. 9 lev radin/Shutterstock.com; p. 11 GRIGORY GALANTNYY/Shutterstock.com; p. 13 Antonin Albert/Shutterstock.com; p. 15 DFree/Shutterstock.com; p. 17 Derya Cakirsoy/Shutterstock.com; p. 19 PeopleImages.com - Yuri A/Shutterstock.com; p. 20 Kostikova Natalia/Shutterstock.com; p. 21 Freebird7977/ Shutterstock.com; p. 23 Mongkolchon Akesin/Shutterstock.com; p. 25 FashionStock.com/Shutterstock.com; p. 27 RossHelen/Shutterstock.com; p. 29 guppyss/Shutterstock.com.

Cataloging-in-Publication Data

Names: Emminizer, Theresa.
Title: Be a fashion designer! / Theresa Emminizer.
Description: Buffalo, NY : PowerKids Press, 2025. | Series: On the job: creative careers | Includes glossary and index.
Identifiers: ISBN 9781499449457 (pbk.) | ISBN 9781499449464 (library bound) | ISBN 9781499449471 (ebook)
Subjects: LCSH: Fashion design–Vocational guidance–Juvenile literature. | Fashion merchandising–Vocational guidance–Juvenile literature. | Fashion–Vocational guidance–Juvenile literature.
Classification: LCC TT507.E49 2025 | DDC 746.9'2023–dc23

Manufactured in the United States of America

Some of the images in this book illustrate individuals who are models. The depictions do not imply actual situations or events.

**CPSIA Compliance Information: Batch #CWPK25. For Further Information contact Rosen Publishing at 1-800-237-9932.**

# CONTENTS

# FABULOUS FASHION

Do you have a **flair** for fashion? Do you love putting together ensembles, or outfits, and **expressing** yourself with style? Do you cut, sew, and create the clothes you want to wear? Do you love to draw? If so, being a fashion designer might be the right career for you!

Fashion designers use their imaginations to create exceptional items for people to wear. They carefully choose the best fabrics, or kinds of cloth, and patterns. They work with teams of people to bring their ideas to life. Fashion design is an exciting trade, but only the best and brightest make it to the top.

Do you have what it takes to be a fashion designer?

# FASHION FIELDS

There are many fields of fashion design. Some designers make one-of-a-kind pieces to be worn by famous movie stars. Others create stylish clothing that can be bought off the rack by ordinary people in a store. Each fashion field has its own set of challenges and opportunities.

**The fashion fields are set apart by several elements:**

- Who the clients, or buyers, are;
- How the clothing is produced, or made;
- The kinds of **materials** that are used; and
- The amount of time and craftsmanship, or skill, that goes into creating the garments, or pieces of clothing.

## LEARNING ON THE JOB!

Fashion trends are popular styles of clothing at certain moments in time. Trend forecasting is predicting, or guessing, what trends will be popular in the future, or times to come.

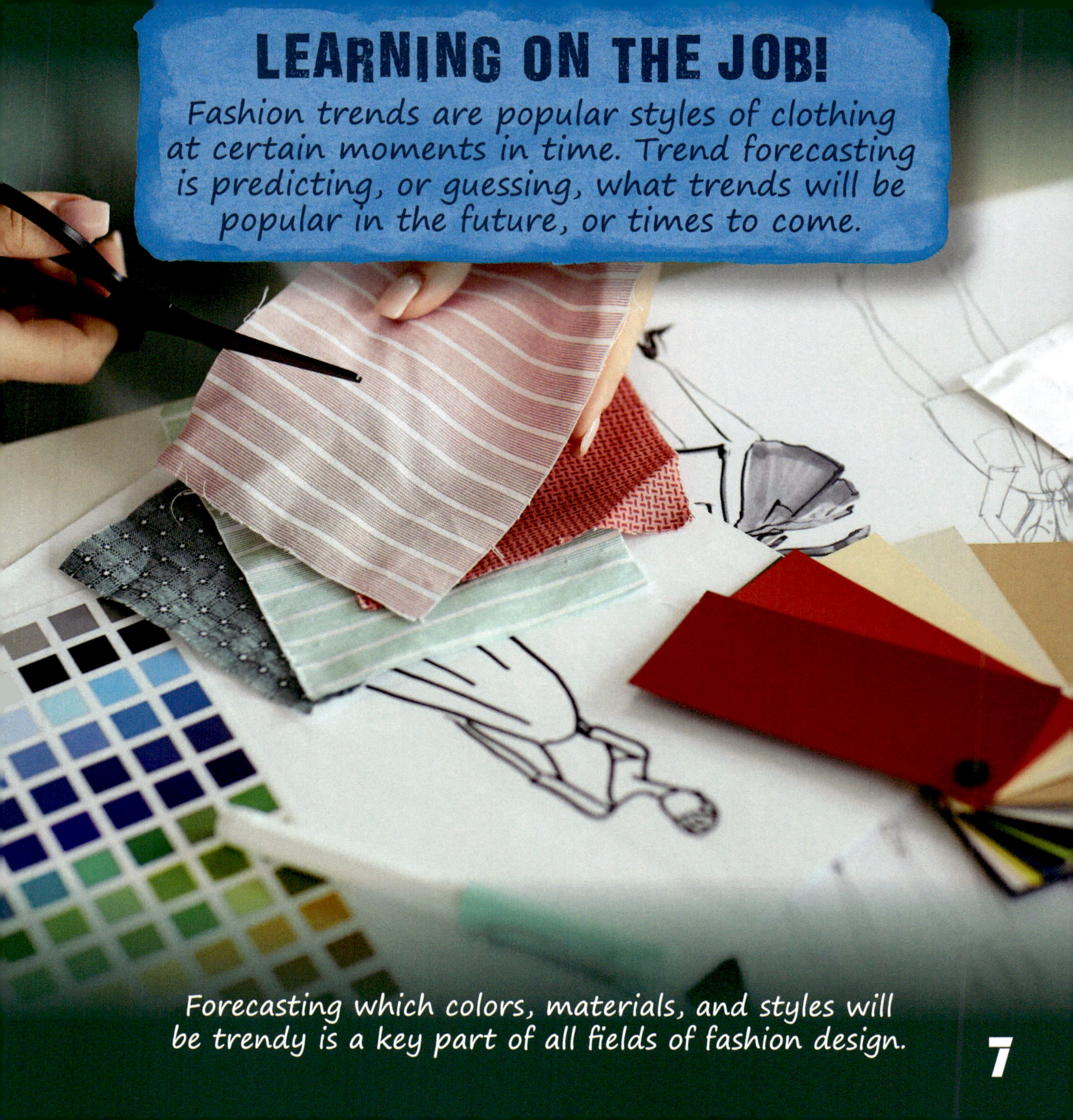

Forecasting which colors, materials, and styles will be trendy is a key part of all fields of fashion design.

# HAUTE COUTURE FASHION

Haute couture fashion is the elite, or top, fashion field. Haute couture designers work for the richest clients. They work closely with clients to understand each's likes, dislikes, style, and body type to create pieces. Custom or bespoke pieces are garments made specially for one person to wear.

Haute couture garments are luxury items. They are made to be artistic rather than practical. Haute couture pieces take hundreds of hours to make. They may feature skillful sewing and **intricate** patterns. They are made of the finest and most expensive, or costly, materials. Haute couture fashion is made for an elite few, but its trends **influence** other fields.

## LEARNING ON THE JOB!

Coco Chanel is one of the most famous haute couture designers of all time. She created elegant, or tasteful, designs that shifted women's fashion away from tight-fitting clothing and to looser styles.

Haute couture designs are often shown on high-end runways. Haute couture is French for "high dressmaking."

# READY-TO-WEAR FASHION

Ready-to-wear fashion is sometimes called prêt-à-porter. Ready-to-wear fashion designers make clothes that can be mass, or widely, produced and sold at stores. Their clothing is made to fit standard sizes rather than custom measurements. It's designed to appeal to lots of different people.

Ready-to-wear fashion designers must mix style with practicality. They must understand who their buyers are and what they're looking for. They often create collections of clothing that can be mixed and matched.

Some haute couture designers, such as Schiaparelli, have ready-to-wear lines of clothing. These lines are lower priced than their haute couture designs and more people can buy them.

Stella McCartney's ready-to-wear fashion line features modern styles that are made in ways that are less harmful to the planet.

## LEARNING ON THE JOB!

Stella McCartney is a leading voice for sustainable, or Earth-friendly, fashion. She carefully chooses materials and her designs are made to be less harmful to the environment, or natural world.

# AVANT-GARDE FASHION

Avant-garde fashion is all about making bold statements. Avant-garde designers challenge people's ideas about beauty and fashion. They experiment, or try new ways of doing things, reimagining **traditional** shapes, forms, materials, and more. Avant-garde designs feature metal, plastic, and other kinds of materials not usually used to make clothing. They may include **technological** aspects, or parts, and be made in unusual ways.

Avant-garde designers must think outside the box. The clothing they create is made to be striking and **extreme**. It cannot be worn practically. Instead, avant-garde fashion is made for show. It explores big ideas and pushes the edges of design.

## LEARNING ON THE JOB!

Iris van Herpen is a Dutch designer who uses 3-D printing and laser cutting to create showstopping pieces that look more like sculptures than clothing. She uses unusual materials to create eye-catching effects.

This 2024 fashion exhibition, or show, at the Musée des Arts Décoratifs in Paris shows designs by Iris van Herpen.

# STREETWEAR

Streetwear is a style of dressing that entered the luxury fashion world more recently. It combines elements of hip-hop, skateboarding, and other urban or city, fashion styles. Traditional luxury brands such as Louis Vuitton now feature streetwear lines and streetwear fashions that can be seen at Paris Fashion Week.

Streetwear fashion designers draw inspiration from sports, music, and club scenes. They create stylish looks that combine comfort and luxury. These pieces usually feature long, loose silhouettes, or shapes, and graphics, such as pictures or words. Streetwear designers need to have a deep understanding of current trends and youth **culture**.

## LEARNING ON THE JOB!

Nigo, a Japanese designer, has been a leading artistic force in the luxury streetwear movement. Nigo is the founder of A Bathing Ape, a popular streetwear brand worn by many famous musicians and celebrities.

Streetwear fashions have been made popular by musicians such as Billie Eilish.

# FASHION EDUCATION

What kind of schooling does someone need to become a fashion designer? Having an associate's (two year) or bachelor's (four year) degree in fashion design or fashion **marketing** can be very helpful. At fashion school, students learn about the principles of design, how to use textiles, or fabrics, and more. They can also build important connections with fashion industry leaders.

Parsons School of Design in New York, New York, is one of the leading fashion schools in the United States. Many famous designers including Marc Jacobs and Tom Ford went there. New York City is considered the fashion capital of America.

Drawing designs, making patterns, and learning to sew are important parts of fashion education.

# HANDS-ON EXPERIENCE

In addition to earning a fashion degree, it's important to get as much hands-on experience in the industry as possible. Beginning fashion designers should seek out internships and apprenticeships at fashion houses. These are jobs in which students and beginners can learn a trade from a **professional**. The right internship can help you build connections within the industry.

Beginning fashion designers must build a portfolio. A portfolio is a collection of drawings and photos that showcase their skills. It should include the best designs and projects a designer has worked on. Having a strong portfolio is a key part of landing a job in the fashion industry.

A portfolio should give employers and clients an idea of who someone is as a designer and what their unique, or one-of-a-kind, style is.

# SPECIAL SKILLS

In addition to earning a fashion degree, working an internship, and building a portfolio, fashion designers need to have special skills. The most important quality for a designer to have is a unique artistic vision, or way of seeing things. A designer's particular style of creativity is what sets them apart. In this field, you can let your imagination run wild!

Designers also need to be good communicators. They need to be able to work well with others, including suppliers, clients, and coworkers. They need to understand market trends. They also need to have business skills to manage their projects well.

Understanding fabrics and having craftsmanship skills are key parts of being a fashion designer.

# WORK ENVIRONMENTS

Fashion designers work in many different settings including design firms, or businesses, clothing companies, theater and dance companies, and more! Fashion designers need room to draw, lay out patterns, and measure and cut fabrics. They may use a dress form or dressmaker's dummy to drape, or hang, fabrics. They also need tools to sew and assemble garments.

Most fashion design jobs can be found in offices in big cities, such as New York or Los Angeles. There, designers may work their way up the fashion ladder by getting a job at a popular fashion house or apparel company. Some fashion designers own their own boutiques, or small stores that sell special collections.

An atelier is a designer's studio, or workroom.

# SCHEDULE AND LIFESTYLE

Being a fashion designer is more of a lifestyle than a job. During busy seasons, fashion designers may work long hours on both weekdays and weekends. They often need to meet hard deadlines, or times when projects need to be completed.

To meet the needs of their clients, a designer's **schedule** needs to be flexible. That means their hours are not set like a traditional nine-to-five job would be. Designers often need to travel to market their designs and meet their clients' needs. Designers must also spend time choosing models, styling models' looks, and making sure that their designs are executed, or completed, properly.

The fashion industry has two big seasons during which new clothing lines are released: spring/summer and autumn/winter.

# SALARY

The world of fashion design can seem very glamorous, or fancy. But how much money does a fashion designer actually make? A fashion designer in the United States can expect to earn a salary, or yearly payment, of around $77,450. Usually salaries for this job range from about $37,480 a year to as much as $130,870.

The amount of money that one earns is based on their level of expertise, or experience and knowledge. It also depends on what brand or fashion house one is employed by. Designers in New York City usually make more money. Happily, the job market for fashion designers is growing!

At this time, there are around 23,800 fashion designers in the United States.

# A PASSION FOR FASHION

From haute couture to ready-to-wear, fashion designers use their imaginations and craftsmanship to create fabulous ensembles for people to wear. Fashion is a form of art. When we choose our clothes, we choose how we express ourselves to the world!

If you have a **passion** for fashion, you might want to become a fashion designer. You don't have to wait until you're a grown-up. Play around with the clothes in your closet to create new outfits! Make your own portfolio of drawings or pictures of designs that you like. Learn to sew or take a design class! Having fun is the best way to spark your creativity.

You could practice your design skills by putting on a fashion show with your friends!

# GLOSSARY

**culture:** The beliefs and ways of life of a certain group of people.

**express:** To communicate what you're thinking or feeling.

**extreme:** Outlandish or very stylized.

**flair:** A knack or skill for something.

**influence:** Power to change or affect someone or something.

**intricate:** Having many parts.

**marketing:** Actions including making people aware of a company's products or services and making sure those products or services are available for purchase.

**material:** Something from which something else can be made.

**passion:** A strong love or liking for something.

**professional:** A person who does a job that requires special training or skills.

**schedule:** A list of times when certain events will or should happen.

**technological:** Having to do with technology, a method that uses science to create useful tools and to solve problems.

**traditional:** Following what's been done for a long time.

# FOR MORE INFORMATION

## BOOKS

Dean, Mary. *Fashion*. Hollywood, FL: Mason Crest, 2022.

Reeves, Diane Lindsey. *Do You Like Keeping Up with Fashion?* Ann Arbor, MI: Cherry Lake Publishing, 2023.

## WEBSITES

**Fashion Kids Magazine**
*www.fashion-kids-magazine.com/blog/sustainable-strides-are-eco-friendly-materials-reshaping-childrens-fashion*
Read about how sustainable materials are changing the world of fashion.

**The New School Parsons**
*www.newschool.edu/parsons/bfa-fashion-design/*
Learn about the fashion design program at The New School Parsons.

# INDEX